Caring for Our
PEOPLE

Carol Greene

CARING FOR OUR EARTH

ENSLOW PUBLISHERS, INC.

Bloy St. & Ramsey Ave.   P.O. Box 38
Box 777   Aldershot
Hillside, N.J. 07205   Hants GU12 6BP
U.S.A.   U.K.

Library of Congress Cataloging-in-Publication Data

Greene, Carol.
    Caring for our people / Carol Greene.
      p. cm.—(Caring for our earth)
    Includes index.
    Summary: Explains, in simple terms, why people are important,
how pollutants and deforestation threaten human existence, and what
children can do to take care of the earth.
    ISBN 0-89490-355-1
    1. Human ecology—Juvenile literature. 2.Pollution—Juvenile
literature. 3. Nature conservation—Juvenile literature.
[1. Human ecology. 2. Pollution. 3. Conservation of natural
resources. 4. Ecology.] I. Title. II. Series: Greene, Carol.
Caring for our earth.
GF48.G727 1991
304.2′8—dc20   91-9235
                                                  CIP
                                                  AC

Printed in the United States of America

10 9 8 7 6 5 4 3 2 1

Photo Credits: Amer-Haitian Bon Zami, Inc., pp. 14, 15 (top), 17, 21, 22,
27; Coalition for the Environment, pp. 6, 8; Margaret Cooper, pp. 10, 11,
15 (bottom), 23; R. Roger Pryor, p. 19; Quinta Scott, p. 25; United
Nations, p. 4.

Cover Photo: James Strawser, University of Georgia, College of
Agriculture, Cooperative Extension Service.

Contents

Hong Kong is a city where many people live.

What Are They?

They need the earth
to stay alive.
The earth gives them
many good things.

Sometimes they take
care of the earth.
Sometimes they don't.
What are they? People.

The family that lives here does not have enough money. Sometimes the children don't get enough to eat.

More than five billion people
live on the earth.
They live in cities and towns,
on farms, in the mountains,
in deserts and on islands,
and many other places.

Some people are rich.
Many have enough money.
But many are so poor
that they are always hungry.
Some even starve to death.

These children are playing a game. People can have fun together.

Why Are People Important?

People are important
because of all they can do.
They can think and feel.
They can laugh and cry.
They can love one another
and they can love the earth.

People are important
because they can help
take care of the earth.

This cat was very sick. But its owner and a vet worked hard to make it well again.

They can plant trees
and gardens and crops.
They can save wild animals
and care for tame animals.
They can keep the earth clean.

People can enjoy the earth.
They can show and tell
how beautiful it is.

They can write poems,
stories, and music
about the earth.
They can dance dances
and paint pictures.

This kangaroo lost its mother. Now people are taking care of it. They even made it a pouch.

People are important
because of all they can do.
But they are also important
just because they are.

Each person is alive.
Each is different.
Each is beautiful,
and each is important.

What Can Happen to People?

If people do not
take care of the earth
and of each other,
bad things can happen.

In Haiti, people
cut down too many trees.
The soil wore away,
and crops could not grow.

There is not much land for growing crops in Haiti.

Now many people in Haiti do not have enough to eat.

In the United States, people put poison wastes in the ground near a town. The wastes got into the soil and the people in the town had to leave their homes.

Many people in Haiti live in homes like these.

Some people in the United States had to leave their homes because of poison wastes in the soil.

HAZARDOUS AREA
DIOXIN
KEEP OUT

In India, some people
made a mistake
at a factory.
Poison gas got into the air
and killed over 2000 people.

In Alaska, a ship
spilled millions of gallons
of oil into the water.
It killed many animals.
Beaches looked ugly and
people felt sad and angry.

People need the earth
for food and homes.
They need clean air
and clean water.

They need beautiful things
to see and love.

But if they do not
take care of the earth,
people will lose these things.

These children need
food, clean water,
clothes, and a home.

What Can We Do?

Some people have already harmed
the earth and one another.
Often they do this
because they are greedy.
They want lots of things.
They don't care about others.

But people can change.
They can think about
the earth and how it works.
They can think about others
and what they need.

People can also think
about all the people
who haven't been born yet.
They should have
a clean, beautiful earth, too.

People must stop putting pollutants
into the air, soil, and water.

Pollutants are harmful things
left over after burning
or making something.
People can make things
in cleaner, safer ways.

People can stop cutting down
too many trees.
They can leave room
for the plants and animals.

People can stop using
so much oil and coal.
They can find other fuels.

If people do these things,
others may lose their jobs.

Then we can help them
find new jobs that
do not harm the earth.

We must also help
poor people now.
We can give them food
and help them find ways
to get their own food.

These children get their only food at school.

These girls in Haiti have no parents. But many people work together to give them healthy, happy lives.

We must help poor people
find ways to earn money
so everyone can live
a healthy, happy life.

Many groups of people
are working together
to make a better earth.
Some work for animals,
some for air, water, or forests,
and some for people.

But they all want
the same thing
—a better earth.

It will take a lot of work
to make the earth better.
All the people in the world
will have to work together.
It will take time and money.
But it will be worth it.

These people are
working for a better
earth by recycling cans.

What Can You Do?

You can help
other people, too.
You can work for
a better earth.
Here are some things
you can do.

1. Learn more about
   the earth and how different
   things work together.
   Get books from the library.
   Watch nature shows on TV.

This boy helps serve food at a place for homeless people.

Talk to your family and friends
about what you have learned.

2. Talk to your family
    or class at school
    about joining a group
    to help a poor child.
    It doesn't cost a lot,
    and it feels great!

3. Write a poem or story,
    draw a picture, sing a song,
    or dance a dance that shows
    how much you love the earth.
    Share what you do
    with other people.

4. Learn about people
   in other countries.
   How are they different from you?
   How are they the same?

5. Be very, very kind
   to the people around you.

These girls are singing for a woman who has helped them.

Words to Know

Alaska—A state northwest of the rest of the United States.

fuel (FYOOL)—Something people burn to get heat or power.

greedy—Wanting to have too much.

Haiti (HATE-ee)—A small island country near Florida.

India—A large country in southern Asia.

oil—A greasy liquid that can be burned as fuel.

poison (POYZ-un)—A thing that is harmful to people, animals, and plants.

soil—A mix of ground-up rock, dead plants and animals, air, and water.

starve—To die from not having food.

waste—A thing left over after burning or making something.

Index

About the Author

Carol Greene is the author of about 100 books for children. She has also worked as a children's editor and a teacher of writing for children. Ms. Greene shares her home with 3 cats and 3 dogs. When her writing and pets allow it, she enjoys gardening, music, and doing volunteer work at her church.